D1458834

Kangaroos

Kangaroos

by Christina Wilsdon

Reader's
Digest

Published by The Reader's Digest Association Limited
London • New York • Sydney • Montreal

CONTENTS

Chapter 1

A kangaroo grows up

DID YOU KNOW?

A mother kangaroo is able to tighten the muscles at the top of her pouch to keep her baby (called a 'joey') safe inside – even while she's hopping at top speed. She relaxes the same muscles to let her joey out.

Kanga-who?

Baby Kangaroo peeks out from his mother's pouch. He has lived tucked inside this warm pocket ever since he was born. At birth, he was no bigger than a bean. He did nothing but drink his mother's milk. As he drank, his body continued to grow.

Now Baby Kangaroo is almost five months old. He is big enough to poke his head out of the pouch and take a look at the world around him. But he will not come all the way out for another month. Until then, he will snuggle in the pouch, bouncing from place to place with his mother as she searches for grass to eat and shady places to rest. And whenever he pokes his head out to look around, he sees how kangaroos behave.

As Mother Kangaroo grazes, Baby Kangaroo leans out of the pouch. He stretches his neck to nibble grass.

One day, Baby Kangaroo pops out of the pouch. He takes a few shaky hops. Then he turns around to go back inside. His mother faces him. She relaxes her pouch so it is wide open. Baby Kangaroo grabs the edge of the pouch and pulls himself in. As he slips into the pocket, he quickly does a somersault. He flips over so his head pokes out in front again and curls up his long tail and feet.

Every day Baby Kangaroo makes a few trips out of the pouch. He grows bigger and stronger. His hops grow steady. He spends more and more time out of the pouch.

Sometimes Baby Kangaroo wanders a little too far away. Then his mother searches for him, clucking loudly. Baby Kangaroo squeaks in reply. He pops back inside her pouch and settles in to drink some milk.

wild WORDS

joey   a baby kangaroo

young-at-foot a joey that is too big to fit in a pouch

buck   a male kangaroo

doe   a female kangaroo

boomers big kangaroo males

fliers another name for big female kangaroos

One day, Baby Kangaroo tries to get back into his mother's pouch — but she pushes him away. He tries again and again, but his mother is firm. She doesn't lean forward to help him to reach into her pouch, and she tightens its opening so he can't crawl in.

Mother Kangaroo keeps Baby Kangaroo out because he has grown too big for her pouch. She must get her pouch ready to hold a new baby. But she is not trying to drive Baby Kangaroo away. He still needs her to care for him and he still drinks her milk. So Mother Kangaroo lets him stick his head inside her pouch to take the milk.

Baby Kangaroo quickly accepts that he must stay outside now. He hops in circles around his mother. He plays with other kangaroos. Baby Kangaroo also likes to tug on his mother's ears. He presses against her as she grooms him from head to toe.

One day Baby Kangaroo will leave his mother's side. He will hop away to find a new place to live. Until then, he will stay very close to her.

Chapter 2

The body of a kangaroo

A mother kangaroo makes
different kinds of milk. A
newborn joey gets very rich
milk. The milk for a young-
at-foot joey is less rich.

The family feature

Some types of kangaroos are as tall as an adult human. Some kinds are no bigger than a rabbit. Some live in deserts, some live on rocks and some live up in trees. But all kinds of kangaroos have one thing in common — the females all have pouches to carry their young. Animals with this special feature are called marsupials (pronounced *mar SOUP ee uls*). A baby marsupial does most of its developing inside its mother's pouch instead of inside her body.

Pocket-size

A baby kangaroo, or joey, doesn't look like a kangaroo when it is born. It is pink and hairless. Its eyes are sealed shut. Its front legs look like flippers with claws. Its hind legs are just tiny stubs. A red kangaroo's joey is only about the size of a jelly bean.

As soon as it is born, the tiny joey creeps over its mother's fur to find her pouch. Once inside the pouch, it starts to drink her milk and keeps drinking for up to four months as it grows and its body takes shape.

Meanwhile, the mother may still be feeding and caring for an older joey.

Cooling and cleaning

A kangaroo's short front legs help it to keep cool. A hot kangaroo licks the skin between its hands and its elbows. This skin has less hair than other parts of its body. It is also rich in blood vessels that are close to the surface.

The kangaroo's licking makes the skin wet. When a breeze blows over the wet skin, it cools the blood by carrying away extra heat. This helps to cool off the kangaroo's whole body.

A kangaroo's front paws are shaped like hands. It uses them to scratch and groom itself, and to hold onto plants.

Kangaroos are plant eaters. Some eat mostly grass. Other kinds, especially the small species, eat mostly leaves.

DID YOU KNOW?

- A kangaroo uses teeth at the front of its mouth to snip off grass and leaves. It has six sharp top teeth and two bottom teeth. When it bites, its bottom teeth press the grass against a tough pad in the top of its mouth. Then its top teeth slice through the blades.

- A kangaroo has strong molars at the back of its mouth to crush and grind food. Over time, they get worn down, and then they fall out and new molars move up to take their place. A kangaroo is very old by the time its supply of molars runs out.

A kangaroo cleans
itself just like a cat
does. It licks its
paws and moves
the paws over its
body to clean and
groom its fur.

A kangaroo's powerful legs and feet make up a third of its entire body weight.

Big foot

Scientists often use the word 'macropod' when describing a kangaroo. Macro means 'big' and pod means 'foot'. So macropod means 'big foot'.

One look at a kangaroo shows that its long hind (back) feet earned it this name. A kangaroo's hind feet are made for motion. Each hind foot has four toes. One toe is very large. This big toe is the main one a kangaroo uses when it hops. A second, shorter toe helps out. The other two toes are joined together and are not used for hopping. They form a comb that the kangaroo uses to groom its fur.

Small kangaroos that live among rocks have rough pads on their feet to help them to grip. A rock wallaby can jump from rock to rock and land on a spot no bigger than a 5p piece without slipping.

Heads up

Kangaroos are always on the alert for danger. Big kangaroos watch out for human hunters and wild dogs, called dingoes. Little kangaroos watch out for these predators, too. They must also worry about cats, foxes, eagles, snakes and big lizards.

A kangaroo's big ears swivel in all directions to listen. Its sensitive nostrils sniff the air. Its big eyes see all around it, like those of a deer. If a kangaroo senses danger, It thumps its feet on the ground to warn others.

Chapter 3

Kangaroos in motion

Trying to make a fast getaway, a kangaroo may leap more than 10 metres – about the length of a bus – in one bound.

DID YOU KNOW?

Female kangaroos are smaller and lighter than males so they are able to hop much faster. That's why female red kangaroos are also called 'fliers'. They move so fast they look like they are flying.

Hippity-hop

What can leap 6 metres with ease and hop over a 2.5 metre fence in a single bound? The world's largest marsupial – the red kangaroo.

The red kangaroo is a hopper, like other kangaroos. A kangaroo does not run like other four-legged animals do. Instead, it tucks up its forelegs and bounces along on its big hind feet. A kangaroo in motion spends most of its time in the air, touching down only on its big hind toes.

A kangaroo can easily hop for hours at a speed of about 20 miles per hour – about the speed of a slow-moving car.

When a kangaroo wants to go faster, it does not hop more often. Instead, it simply makes its hops longer and covers more ground with each hop.

A kangaroo's body gives it an extra boost by saving energy from each hop to use for the next hop. Each leg has tough, stretchy cords in it called tendons. Tendons attach muscles to bones. They also store some of the energy that is created with each hop. The stored energy helps a kangaroo to take its next hop, just as a diving board helps you to jump higher when you bounce on it before you dive. Scientists often liken kangaroos to pogo sticks.

Multi-tasking tails

A kangaroo's tail also helps it to get around. Watch a kangaroo hop, and you will see its tail bounce up and down as it moves. Tendons in the top of the tail store energy from its hops just as tendons in the legs do. The tail also helps to balance the front of its body. As if that were not enough, the bouncing tail even helps a hopping kangaroo to breathe. It works like a pump to help the animal to breathe in and out quickly as it hops.

The tail also acts like a rudder when a kangaroo hops, helping it to change direction in mid air.

The tail comes in handy when a kangaroo wants to 'bunny-jump', or move forward without hopping. First, the kangaroo leans forward and puts its front feet on the ground. Then it moves its tail behind them. It leans on its front legs and its tail as it swings both hind legs forward at the same time to take another step.

When a kangaroo stands up, it leans on its tail and uses it like a third leg.

Walk ways

A swimming kangaroo can kick each hind leg separately. But on land, a kangaroo always moves its hind legs together when it hops or bunny-jumps. Scientists don't know the reason why.

A tree kangaroo, however, can do what other kangaroos cannot. It can walk on all four feet – but only when it walks along branches or leaps from limb to limb. When it is on the ground, a tree kangaroo hops.

Forward gear only

A kangaroo's long, strong tail is so big that it stops the kangaroo from moving backwards.

Chapter 4

Kangaroos together

Kangaroos would rather run than fight. They don't mind sharing their grazing land with sheep or cattle or other mobs of kangaroos. They don't defend a territory.

The roo crew

A kangaroo mob does not have a leader. It seems to be just a gathering of kangaroos that happen to live in the same area. A mob may have as few as three kangaroos or as many as a hundred.

Even though there are no leaders, some male kangaroos do boss around other males. Scientists call them the dominant kangaroos. A dominant male kangaroo may try to keep other males away from the females.

Kangaroos that live on Australia's grassy plains often form mobs. Being in a mob helps to keep a kangaroo safe because there are more eyes, ears and noses to be on the alert for danger. If a predator startles the mob, the kangaroos flee in all directions. This explosion of hopping may confuse the predator so much that it cannot catch a single kangaroo.

Kangaroos that live in forests tend to live alone, except when they have young.

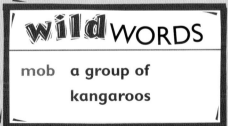

wildWORDS

mob	a group of kangaroos

Fisticuffs!

Most of the time, kangaroos live quietly. They rest during the heat of the day and feed in the cool of night. But sometimes, male kangaroos turn into kick boxers.

A male may fight to show that he is dominant. A dominant male is the one who will mate with the females. Fights often break out when a female is ready to mate again. Kangaroo fights are often called sparring.

Before a male starts sparring, he threatens another male. This threat is a warning that means 'scram'! A grey kangaroo sends his warning by pulling up grass or scraping the ground, then rubbing his chest in the scrape. A red kangaroo may strut around another male, moving on tiptoe and keeping his side turned towards the rival.

If this doesn't work, the kangaroo stands up tall and punches the other male with his forelegs. If the other male punches back, the two begin sparring.

Each kangaroo twists his head back to protect his eyes while boxing with his paws. The two males also kick each other. They lean on their tails, lift their hind legs, and kick at each other's bellies. The fight ends when one kangaroo simply gives up and goes away.

Showman

This big, red kangaroo buck shows off his muscular body every chance he can. It's his way of letting other males know that he is the 'old man', the dominant kangaroo.

Sparring kangaroos protect their eyes by twisting their heads back, away from the action.

A mother kangaroo raises her joeys without any help. The joeys are either in her pouch or near her all day and all night.

Kangaroo families

Who raises baby kangaroos? It's the mothers, the does. Male kangaroos do not have pouches and don't help the females to raise their joeys.

A kangaroo doe can handle it. She may even have three babies of different ages all at the same time. One baby is the youngster hopping at her heels. Tucked inside her pocket is a younger joey, who is still attached to a teat and growing. The third is inside her body and has not yet been born. It will not grow big enough to be born until the joey in the pouch is out and about.

How long a joey stays with its mother depends on which kind of kangaroo it is. A red kangaroo joey, for example, stays with its mother for a year and a half. A black-striped wallaby baby stays with its mother for less than a year.

Walla-walla-who?

Some species of kangaroos are known as wallaroos and wallabies. Wallaroos look like the familiar red and grey kangaroos but are slightly smaller. Wallabies are smaller still, ranging from only 30 centimetres to just over a metre. The larger wallabies also look like the big kangaroos, but they are thicker and have more fur.

Chapter 5

Kangaroos in the world

Red kangaroos, the tallest species, live in dry, almost desert areas and have to travel long distances for food and water.

Kinds of kangaroos

About 55 different kinds, or species, of kangaroo hop around Australia and the nearby island of New Guinea. They are all part of the macropod family.

The six biggest macropods are sometimes called 'the great kangaroos'. The western grey kangaroo is one of the six. It lives in dry scrublands and forests. It grazes at night and rests under trees during the day. The other great kangaroos are the eastern grey kangaroo, the red kangaroo and three species that are called wallaroos.

Scientists place rat kangaroos, potoroos and bettongs in a related but separate family, called potoroids (pronounced *POT oh royds*). They look more like rodents than kangaroos.

Climbing roos

Tree kangaroos live in rainforests. A tree kangaroo's front legs are almost as long as its back legs. But its hind feet are not enormous like other kangaroos' feet are. It walks easily along branches as it looks for leaves to eat. But on the ground, it hops.

Kangaroo cousin

Wallabies are smaller than the great kangaroos. Some wallabies look like their larger cousins and live in grassy woodlands. This yellow-footed rock wallaby lives among rocks and looks different from other wallabies.

Kangaroo habitats

Over time, kangaroos and their relatives have adapted to almost every habitat in Australia and New Guinea – from deserts to rainforests. Red kangaroos live in dry places and grasslands with a few shady trees to rest under. Grey kangaroos live in woodlands with open space for grazing.

Steep desert rock cliffs are home to rock wallabies, which get all the water they need from the plants they eat. The tree kangaroo is adapted to the rainforest. Even its fur is parted so that the rain can stream away off its back.

FAST FACTS ABOUT RED KANGAROOS

SCIENTIFIC NAME	*Macropus rufus*
CLASS	Mammals
ORDER	Diprotodontia
SIZE	Males up to 1.8 metres tall Females up to 1.2 metres tall
WEIGHT	Males to 90 kilograms Females to 35 kilograms
LIFE SPAN	18 years in the wild 25 years in captivity
HABITAT	Dry grasslands near scattered trees
TOP SPEED	About 30 miles per hour

Where kangaroos live

The yellow areas show where kangaroos live.

New Guinea

IRIAN JAYA (INDONESIA)

PAPUA NEW GUINEA

AUSTRALIA

MARSUPIALS GALORE!

Australia and the islands around it are home to many kinds of marsupials. Kangaroos are marsupials, but so are koala bears, Tasmanian devils, numbats, wombats, opossums, bandicoots and bilbies. More than 100 species of marsupial can be found living here and nowhere else in the world. There are also more than 60 species of opossum living in Central and South America, and one in the USA.

There are so many kangaroos in Australia that kangaroo 'crossing' signs are posted along roads to warn drivers to stay alert. These signs are even posted in the suburbs of large cities.

The future of kangaroos

Millions of red and grey kangaroos live in Australia. The native Aborigines have always hunted them for food. When Europeans first arrived in the 1600s, they marvelled at kangaroos. Then they, too, used kangaroos as food.

But when Europeans started farming in Australia, they began to view kangaroos as enemies. They considered that the kangaroos were taking the food and water that their sheep should have instead. So they began shooting large numbers of kangaroos.

Today, red and grey kangaroos are still hunted to control their population. This hunt is controlled by law. Only a certain number may be killed each year. The kangaroos' meat is used for food and their skins for leather. Some people even think that ranchers should replace their sheep with kangaroos.

The big kangaroos are not endangered, but many small species are. The cutting down of rainforests removes habitat for tree kangaroos. Cats and foxes, which the Europeans first brought to Australia many years ago, often kill small kangaroos. Today, some small species live only in protected areas or on islands.

Many people are working to help endangered kangaroos by protecting their habitat. That way, there will always be a place for kangaroos and the other marvellous marsupials of Australia.

GLOSSARY OF WILD WORDS

boomer	a big male kangaroo	macropod	the scientific name for the kangaroo that means 'big foot'
buck	a male kangaroo	marsupial	a mammal whose young are born after a very short time in the body and then grow inside a pocket on the mother's stomach
dingo	a species of wild dog in Australia		
doe	a female kangaroo		
flier	a big female kangaroo	mob	a group of kangaroos
habitat	the natural environment where an animal or plant lives	pouch	a warm pocket on a female kangaroo's stomach that holds a joey
joey	a baby kangaroo		

predator	an animal that hunts and eats other animals to survive	wallaby	a marsupial related to the kangaroo but much smaller
roo	a nickname for any large kangaroo	young-at-foot	a joey that is too big to fit in its mother's pouch but is still in her care
sparring	fighting between male kangaroos		
species	a group of living things that are the same in many ways		
wallaroo	slightly smaller type of kangaroo		

INDEX

CREDITS

Kangaroos is an *All About Animals* fact book
published by The Reader's Digest Association, Inc.

Written by Christina Wilsdon

Copyright © 2006 The Reader's Digest Association, Inc.
This edition was adapted and published in 2008 by
The Reader's Digest Association Limited
11 Westferry Circus, Canary Wharf, London E14 4HE
Reprinted in 2010

Editor: Rachel Warren Chadd
Designer: Nicola Liddiard
Art editor: Simon Webb

We are committed both to the quality of our products and the service we provide
to our customers. We value your comments, so please do contact us on
08705 113366 or via our website at www.readersdigest.co.uk

If you have any comments or suggestions about the content of our books,
email us at gbeditorial@readersdigest.co.uk

Printed in China

ISBN: 978 0 276 44321 3
Book code: 640-004 UP0000-2
Oracle code: 504500064H.00.24